Offensive Line Manual

Introduction

 # Introduction

I, like most coaches, have worked hard to listen to people I respect and attempt to take little nuggets from those willing to give. Now, I have the opportunity to give back and I hope this offensive system can be of help to you in your journey as a coach. Feel free to take any part of this offense that can help you, but I feel what makes it work is the entire system.

We have worked hard to continue to grow it and work through the problems that can come from blending different worlds.

The entire system can be found on Coachtube.com:

There is also more information on my website: FBCoachSimpson.com.

This book is also the 4th in a series of books that can be found on Amazon or FBCoachSimpson.com.

 # Introduction

I firmly believe that the most unselfish position in all of sports is the offensive line. In all other sports each person can touch the ball or to gain the glory. This is the one last purely unselfish position we have in most athletic events.

So, I hold a special place in my heart for the linemen I have coached over the past 18-seasons. It is also one of the toughest positions to coach and most important ones for a team's success. The game is easy when you are winning up front and very difficult when you are not.

I hope this book gives some tips and tools to your program as you work to win in the trenches. My goal was not to only give drills that would work in my system, but in all gap-scheme type offenses. Best of luck as you go through this material, and feel free to reach out if I can help in other areas.

 # Introduction

This book is a supplement to the Gun T RPO offensive system. The plan in this book is to go how we coach our offensive line – from philosophy to personnel choices to drills to game plan.

These drills fit very well with what we do on offense, although many are drills that could work with most "gap-scheme" offensives schemes. As with everything in football, I learned from many great coaches and tried to make this into a clean and easy to understand system.

I am very appreciative of the support and in no way do I have all the answers, but I have learned a few things along the way and I hope some of them can help you in your journey. This offense has been very good to me and I hope to see it help other coaches.

"A good leader is always learning. The great leaders start learning young and continue until their last breath." – Bill Walsh

Recommendations

Quotes

"Coach Simpson's offensive system is simply one of the best out there. Coach does a phenomenal job of explaining his offense in detail. I've always been a power spread coach but there was just something about this system that made me want to learn more. This is truly the best of both worlds in the wing-t and spread blended together. This season we took over a program that had been spread the last three years with a division 1 QB, and two division 1 WRs. We were taking over a team that returned 1 TD from the year before and no offensive starters. We decided to install this offense with almost no summer install work and ended up averaging over 30 points and just over 350 yards per game. Lastly, this system is very adaptable to fit your kids strengths year in and year out. I highly recommend checking out Kenny Simpson's Gun-T Offense." - Coach Lucas Stanton

"Coach Simpson has done it again. Our staff has used his previous material and have become better coaches for it. Coach Simpson's ability to break complex concepts into smaller parts is excellent. His material is perfect for any coach that wants to become better at his craft." – Coach Joel Brose

Quotes

"Coach Simpson's Gun T Offensive Overview is an excellent offensive resource. This course provides the foundation of Coach Simpson's offensive philosophy. Coach believes in the monikers that "Less is More" and the "Rule of 3", which both were evident in the explanation of the offense. His explanations were clear and concise, and the presentations were easy to follow." - Todd Knipp

"This is absolutely amazing. Coach Simpson does an excellent job of explaining his system. Whether you're a young coach or an experienced coach this is must see. You can easily see why he is a successful coach. His detailed organization is on point and I cannot wait to learn more from Coach Simpson." - Mike Kloes

"I've been following coach Simpson for a while now and it's very clear to me that even though I may not be a HC, we have similar philosophies. If you are a Wing T guy looking for ways to "Modernize" your offense, or a Spread guy looking for an effective and efficient run game this is the offense you should be looking at!" - Coach Sheffer

Quotes

"Most offensive systems you must have really good players to run them, but with Coach Simpson's 'Gun-T' RPO system, you can be very successful just manipulating defenses with the X's & O's." - Steven Swinson, Indiana Wesleyan University

"As a traditional wing T coach for over 30 years I was looking for a package to add to my offense in order to force defenses to defend width and depth. Coach Simpson's Gun-T RPO offense does exactly that with the built in "what if then" RPO's and RRO's." - Coach Brissette

"The Gun T RPO System really helped us evolve our wing T offense and really put defenses in conflict. This system helped us break a 20-game losing streak and finish with a winning record for the first time since 2014." -Tom Mulligan, Head Coach Elmwood Park High School, Elmwood Park, New Jersey

 # Table of Contents

Belief System

I firmly believe games are won and lost in the trenches. The offensive line is the last line of selfless play in most major sports. These players literally lay their body on the line for others to be successful. This group will lead the team to victory most seasons if they will have a few characteristics I will detail in this book.

While most of this book will be focused on technique, play design and personnel choices, none of this will matter if the line does not possess these qualities:

Hard Work – Nothing will take the place of a player that will work as hard as any opponent.

Being Coachable – The job of our staff is to improve our worst players and our best players. We want our linemen to know you have NEVER "arrived". Be willing to be coached.

Nastiness – Being a gentleman off the field is awesome, but when you cross the line you are fighting every play for your family, have that mindset. Protect our team.

Ability to learn concepts – We want linemen that know what we are trying to accomplish, not just "block that guy". Know the "why" of each block and play. Work smart and hard.

"Success demands singleness of purpose." - Vince Lombardi

 # Grading System

We are very simple in our grading system with our offensive linemen. A simple +/- is given for effort and technique. We will breakdown each play and give the mark. While the grade is equally calculated we value effort over technique every day of the week.

We stress to our linemen that the technique helps, but never replaces great effort. We want to make sure we reward blocks of great effort and will often give "bonus" points in the grading scale to those that show great effort.

Personnel

 # Personnel Choices

When you are designing any offense it should always adapt and evolve to your players skill set. While I love certain plays, each season our "best" play rotates depending on what our personnel looks like. Working with scheme is fun, but football is not played on a whiteboard and your X's may be better or worse than their O's at certain skills. The great offensive coaches are always able to highlight the skill set of their players and hide their deficiencies as much as possible.

In this section, I will give you the "optimal" skills each position has. Understand that if you do not have each position, you can still run the system, but I'd recommend highlighting specific parts. I refer to a few of those in the "IF-THEN" section later in this book.

As a coach be sure to constantly evaluate your players and find their strengths. In the Gun-T RPO system there are multiple spots that can have different skill sets, but a few key ones that you want to place your "better" players.

 # Strong-Quick

We run a QUICK and STRONG SIDE

--We rarely have 5-6 good offensive linemen

--We wanted to have spots for guys that were too slow for traditional Wing-T spots

This also makes our line only learn plays one way

--Easier to install plays

--More time to work on types of blocks each specific position uses

--IE -- Strong tackles NEVER PULL or REACH in our system

 # Cross Training

While we do our best to develop depth at every position, we understand that that may not be the case in a given year. To help with this we will "cross-train" our athletes in multiple positions.

Generally, this is done with our next best linemen. While we would love to have a backup at each spot, often we are realistically trying to get 2-3 backups ready. We will work one guard as the main backup, have a backup center (who may be a starter at another position) and a backup tackle.

In another section in this book, I walk through our full practice schedule. Here is the small part of the practice schedule that we attempt to work all linemen in different positions.

PD	QB	T	Y/B	X and A	OL	DL	ILB	OLB	DB	
1	SPECIALTY PERIOD --- DC with Non-specialty defensive players --- OL Coach with all linemen not involved									
2	Coach With Kicker, Coach With PAT Group, Coach With Punter/Snapper, Coach With Returnmen									
3	SPECIAL TEAMS GROUP - ROTATE THROUGH MAIN 4 -- Steal time for QB/OL -- Steal time for DL/ILB or DB/OLB									
4										
5										Crossover
6										
7	BREAK					BREAK				

 # Personnel Choices

When running this offense there are a few "non-negotiable" parts you absolutely must have. But most of the time there are players with the required skills at each position. As coaches we must adapt our offense to the players we have. That being said, there are a few qualities you should search for at each position.

This book is geared for the offensive line, however the F, Y and B are heavily involved in the blocking scheme so I am including them in this section.

F - This should be your best athlete. By design this position will touch the ball the most of any spot (except the QB position). It is easy to get them the ball in space (empty/screens) or simply run the ball (buck/belly). As with every position, you must adapt to their skill set, but this needs to be your best player.

If this player is a solid blocker it will open much more in the run game. We want him to be able to lead on second level players and pass protect.

B - This is the hardest position to find and the most important one. It will cause you to adjust what you do offensively to fit his skill set. I'd attempt to use your second-best player if he is able/willing to block and put him in this position. Size will matter at this spot, since he will be asked to down block defensive ends and linebackers. If he is gritty, but undersized there are some adjustments that can be made, but he must be effective blocking.

The second part of his job is as important. We want this player to be a good runner – if he is very athletic we will run jet and counter with him. He also needs to be able to catch at least short passes or play action passes. In my opinion, other than the QB, this position will dictate how much you use certain formations and plays.

In short, if he struggles with blocking, it will require adjustments in running buck and possibly belly/duo.

Personnel Choices

Y – Tight-end. Must be able to block defensive lineman. His job is crucial on buck. We generally pick our 3rd guard for this spot. If he has the ability to catch the ball that is great, but he must be a willing and able blocker for this offense to work.

Often this player is our 6th best linemen, although as I have seen through experience, if you have a dominant TE it will allow you to run more of your base offense without needing to make adjustments.

QG – Most important lineman on the team. He needs to be your most athletic player on the line. Size is secondary. He will be pulling on almost all strong side runs. When you decide who goes where, start at this position.

SG – Second most important lineman on the team. He will pull kick most of the time, but needs to be athletic enough to wrap for Quick Belly. Usually the stronger, not as athletic of the two guards.

QT – Next most important lineman. What his skill set brings to the table will allow you (or not) to run to the quick side and all your RPO game on the backside. He also needs to be able to get in space on screen and get to second level on RPO game.

C – Must be very consistent at snapping for the offense to run smoothly. Usually this is a smart kid that can call the fronts and is able to handle backside blocking. If he is not as great a blocker, we can give help, but if he is a solid blocker it makes the scheme much easier to achieve.

ST – Usually this is a very physical, but not as athletic tackle. Often for us this is our biggest lineman. If he played at the college level he would have to play guard since often these types of bodies struggle with speed. Must be able to down block, double team and cut/hinge on backside runs.

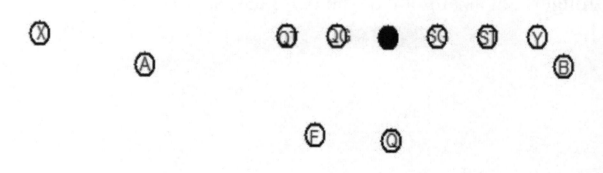

Base Alignment

Position	Alignment
X	Top of the numbers
A	Split X and QT off the ball
F	Heels on QB toes. Split the QG and QT
Y	Head even with hip of center. 2 ft splits
B	2x2 off Y
QT	Head even with hip of center. 2 ft splits
QG	Head even with hip of center. 2 ft splits
C	On Ball
SG	Head even with hip of center. 2 ft splits
ST	Head even with hip of center. 2 ft splits
Q	Heels at 5 yards

Theory

This offense operates with what I call the "rule of three". We attempt to limit the areas of the field we attack into three concepts or less. In this playbook you will see:

3 strong side run plays
3 quick side run plays
3 flood concepts
2 play action concepts
3 screen concepts
3 RPO concepts
3 slow screen concepts
1 drop back (that's right just 1) concept

Simple is the key in this offense. We want to just "tag" each run, screen, RPO or flood concept to take advantage of the defense. Then when you mix in some motion and formations, it becomes much more difficult for a defense. The main objective is to only use a motion/formation/tag for a specific purpose, not simply to look complex. If they are not stopping your base plays, don't stop yourself by calling something else!

The offensive line in our offense is asked to learn the base plays and the concepts. Our goal is to learn the concept so well that we can make quick adjustments and use "tags".

Formations

Formations

We attempt to keep formation simple for our players, and they are VERY SIMPLE for our offensive line. We run a Quick and Strong side if we know we are going to attach a "Y" for over 80% of our snaps that season.

By running a Quick and Strong side we are able to choose personnel that matches the skills needed at each position, it also allows us to hide deficiencies that our linemen may have.

Once our Linemen hear "Red or Blue" they instantly know where to line up. The other tags only speak to our other players. This makes it very simple for them.

If you'd like a full compliment of play you can get the playbook from FBCoachSimpson.com/downloads.

Red

X   QT   QG   C   SG   ST   Y

A   B

F

Q

Position	Alignment
X	Top of the numbers
A	Split X and QT off the ball
F	Heels on QB toes. Split the QG and QT
Y	Head even with hip of center. 2 ft splits
B	2x2 off Y
QT	Head even with hip of center. 2 ft splits
QG	Head even with hip of center. 2 ft splits
C	On Ball
SG	Head even with hip of center. 2 ft splits
ST	Head even with hip of center. 2 ft splits
Q	Heels at 5 yards

Blue

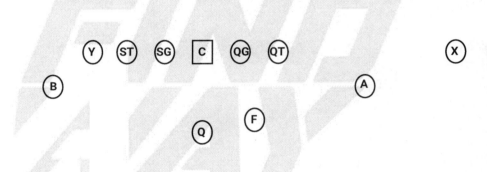

Position	Alignment
X	Top of the numbers
A	Split X and QT off the ball
F	Heels on QB toes. Split the QG and QT
Y	Head even with hip of center. 2 ft splits
B	2x2 off Y
QT	Head even with hip of center. 2 ft splits
QG	Head even with hip of center. 2 ft splits
C	On Ball
SG	Head even with hip of center. 2 ft splits
ST	Head even with hip of center. 2 ft splits
Q	Heels at 5 yards

Base Plays

Base Plays

This manual is not a playbook, but it is important that a coach understand the base plays we are trying to be experts at in our offense to understand the drills and manual.

The following pages will be our base plays in our offense. We are a "series" based offense – which means we want our backfield action to look the same on multiple plays to cause deception. If you'd like more information on this, I'd recommend the playbook or other materials available at Fbcoachsimpson.com.

In this section you will see our base rules for Buck, Belly, Counter, Jet and Quick Belly as well as our roll out protection.

Our entire RPO game only involves our Quick Tackle. He is the only player that must listen for an adjustment to his blocking scheme on most plays.

In the following pages I will walk through how our rules-based blocking will handle all fronts.

Buck

Buck
Base Rules

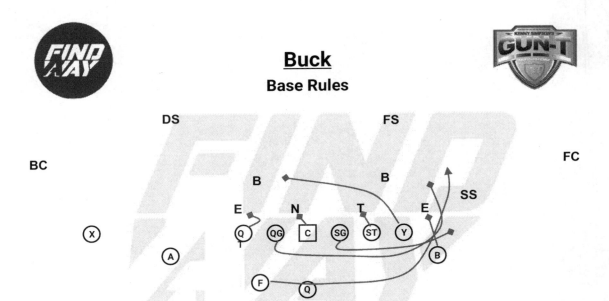

Position	Job Description
X	
A	
F	Cross QB's face for 2 steps, find quick guard and get hand on his back
Y	Gap/Down/Backer
B	Gap/Down/Backer
QT	Step Hinge or Cut
QG	Pull Wrap
C	On/Backside
SG	Pull Kick
ST	Gap/Down/Backer
Q	

Buck

4-3

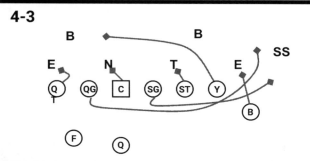

4-2

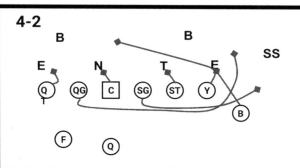

Under

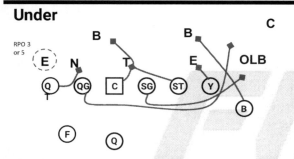

5-2

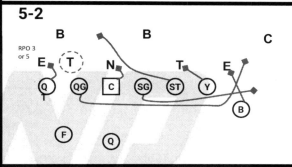

3-3

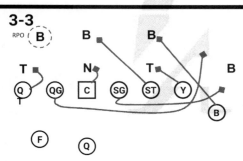

Stay Call= A & B gaps covered or 3

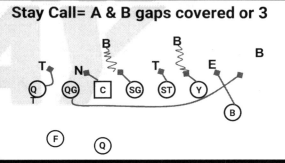

RPO's off Buck

"Read and Bogo"
QB reads the 5 tech. Can throw bubble post snap

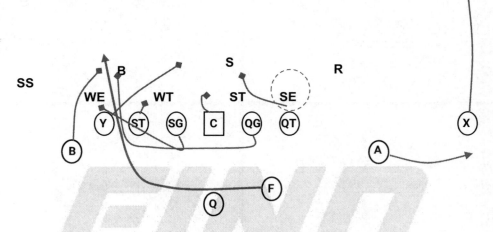

"Steal"
QB reads the 4i/3 tech

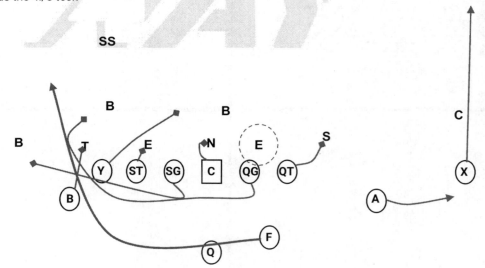

Belly

Belly
Base Rules

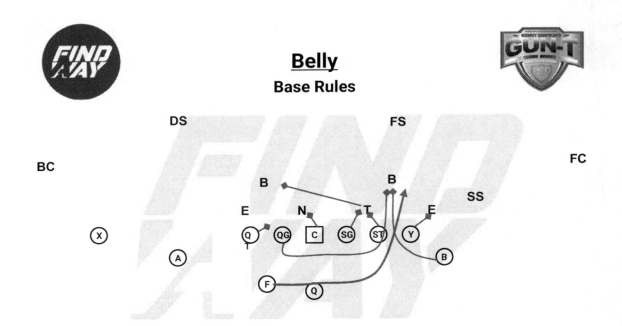

Position	Job Description
X	
A	
F	Slide step to the QB, attack downhill behind pulling guard
Y	Block out
B	Fold inside to playside LB
QT	Step-hinge unless RPO
QG	Wrap to first daylight. Eyes inside
C	On/Backside
SG	#1 Defensive Lineman
ST	#2 Defensive Lineman. If #2 is outside Y, then DBL to backside LB
Q	

4-3

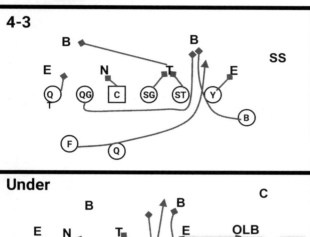

4-2

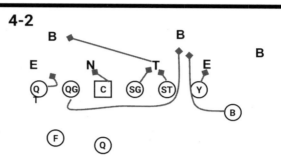

Under

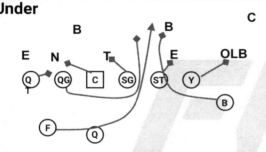

5-2

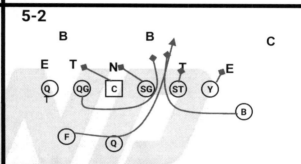

3-3

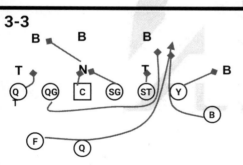

"Fan" Tells wing to block OLB

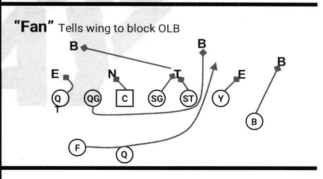

"Switch" If wide OLB, Y and B can switch

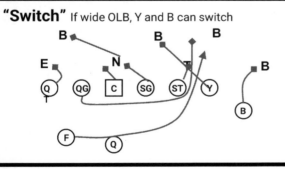

Counter

Counter
Base Rules

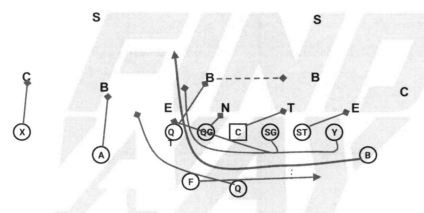

Position	Job Description
X	Block #1
A	Block #2
F	"Take" ball and give underneath carry out fake
Y	Pull Wrap
B	Counter and depth step, get ball under F
QT	Gap/Down/Backer- Work path, if playside backer flys out, don't chase, take backside
QG	Gap/Down/Backer
C	Gap/Down/Backer
SG	Pull Kick
ST	Step Hinge
Q	Give ball and block edge

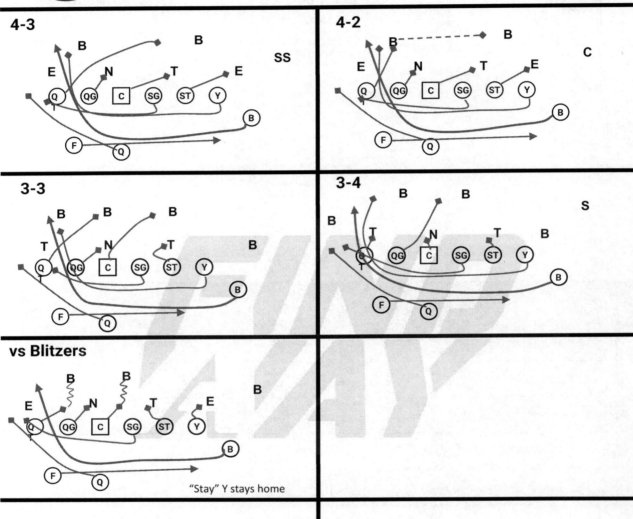

4-3

4-2

3-3

3-4

vs Blitzers

"Stay" Y stays home

Jet

Jet

Jet Motion Overview

In keeping with the series-based offense, the Gun T RPO system uses "jet motion" and marries the following plays:

-Jet Sweep
-Quick Belly
-Quick Belly-Read
-Trips Passes
-Throwback Pass
-F Draw

This attacks the defense in every place with the same backfield action. The jet motion is difficult to adjust to as the offense transitions quickly into a 3 x 1 look. Then with the different run-pass plays built into the offense, it becomes very difficult for the defense to stop.

Each play can be run independently from the motion, but when you pair them together it gives a much more "series like" approach that is difficult to defend.

For the Offensive Line Manual, I have included our two base runs – Jet/Quick Belly and our roll-out protection.

Jet
Base Rules

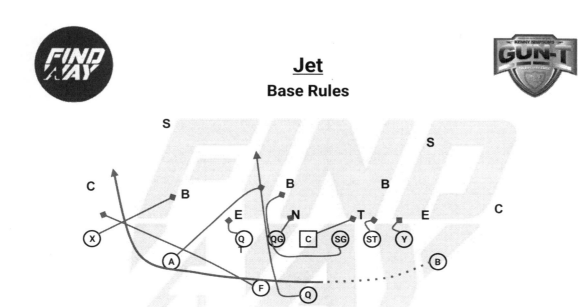

Position	Job Description
X	Crack OLB
A	Chip 5 tech if needed, crack ILB
F	Take flat path and kick first defender to show. If no one shows, wrap to corner
Y	Step inside, hinge
B	Quick Motion on Q signal, cut off F
QT	Hook DE
QG	Block #1 DL, Hook 3 tech
C	On/Backside
SG	Wrap through first gap on quickside, eyes inside
ST	Step inside, hinge
Q	Hand or toss to B

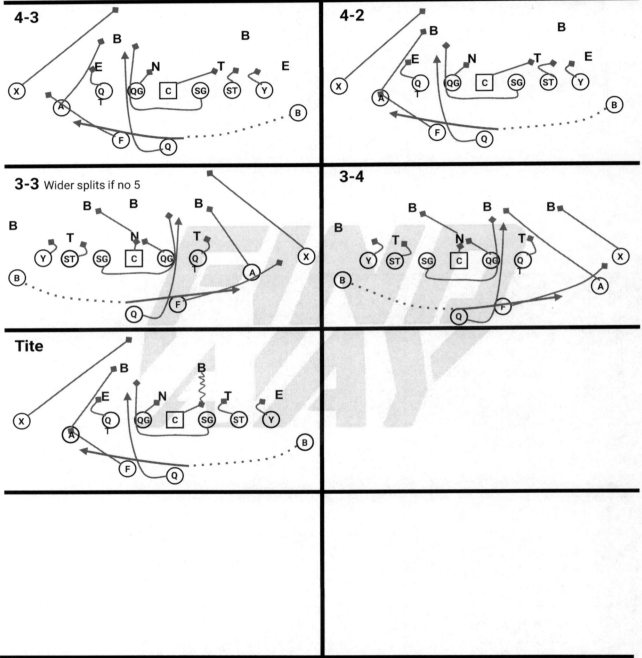

4-3

4-2

3-3 Wider splits if no 5

3-4

Tite

Quick Belly

Quick Belly
Base Rules

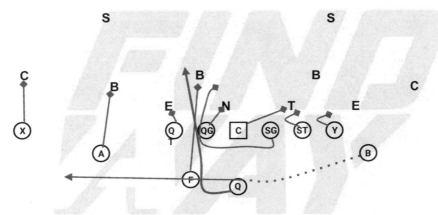

Position	Job Description
X	RPO if no motion. If motion block #1
A	RPO if no motion. If motion block #2
F	Lead on ILB (Play side)
Y	Step in, hinge
B	If motion, fake jet. No motion, step hinge
QT	#2 DL Block out, if aligned inside, take in
QG	#1 DL
C	On/Backside
SG	Wrap first gap quick side, look inside
ST	Step in, hinge
Q	Slide step, and get downhill

Quick Belly

4-3

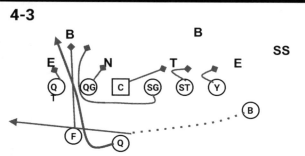

4-2

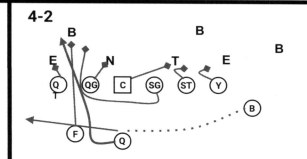

3-3 QT take where he wants to go

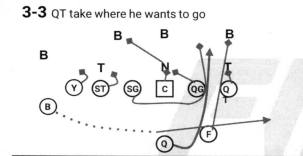

3-4

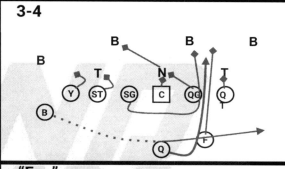

Tite

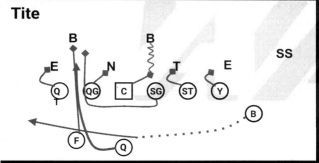

"Fan" Tells "F" block OLB

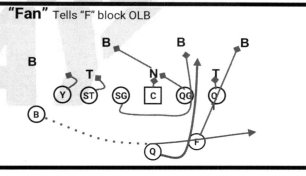

Roll Out Protection

Rodeo/Lasso
Base Rules vs 4 Down

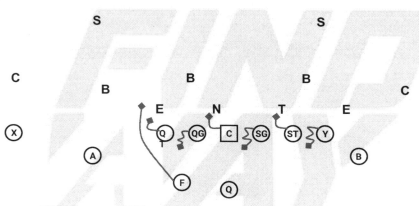

Position	Job Description
X	Route
A	Route
F	Attack outside edge, seal DE or find ILB on edge
Y	Check gap, if no pressure stay square (If not in route)
B	Route
QT	Reach end
QG	Check gap, if no pressure stay square
C	Reach 1 tech
SG	Check gap, if no pressure, hinge back
ST	Reach 3 Tech
Q	Attack edge and fit off "F" block

Rock/Load
Base Rules vs 4 Down

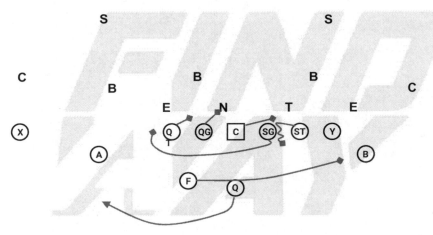

Position	Job Description
X	Route
A	Route
F	Play fake and block DE/OLB
Y	Check gap, if no pressure stay square (If not in route)
B	Route
QT	Block back, gap protect
QG	Block back, gap protect
C	Block back, gap protect
SG	Pull with depth and attempt to log
ST	Inside hinge
Q	Fake to F and roll out

Rollout Protections vs 3 Down

Rodeo/Lasso

Playside stay square. Block gap
Backside block gap, if no show hinge with depth

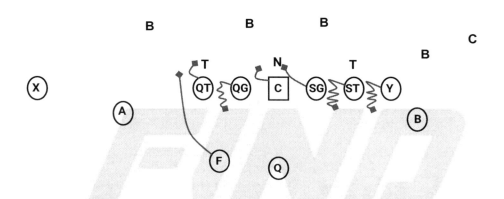

Rock/Load

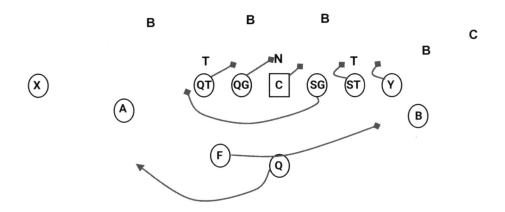

Slow Screens

Rocket
Base Rules

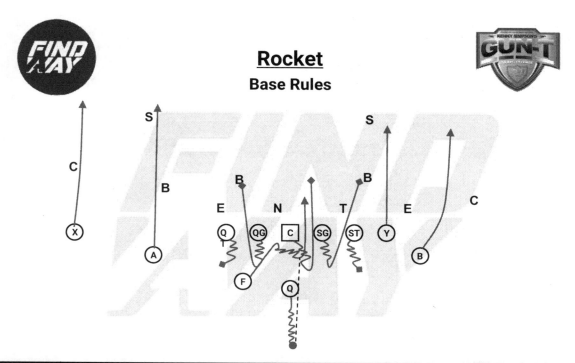

Position	Job Description
X	Go route
A	Go route
F	Step up for 2 counts, run away from any DL
Y	Go route
B	Go route
QT	Pass protect
QG	Show Pass for 1 count, then release to ILB
C	Show pass for 1 count, then release to most dangerous linebacker
SG	Show pass for 1 count, then release to ILB
ST	Pass protect
Q	Bail 3 steps and sit, then fade back to draw rush

Laser

Base Rules
Like vs aggressive DE

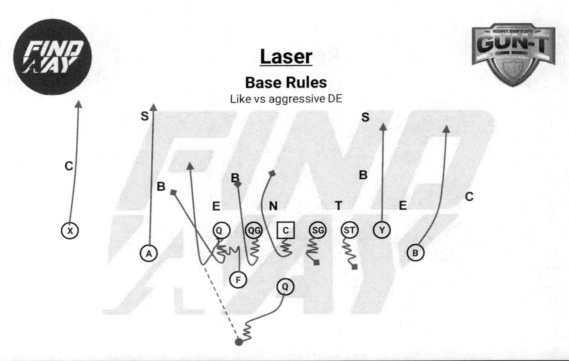

Position	Job Description
X	Go route
A	Go route
F	Attack edge for 1 count, then drift wide
Y	Go route
B	Go route
QT	Show pass for 1 count, then kick OLB
QG	Show Pass for 1 count, then release to ILB
C	Show pass for 1 count, then release to backside ILB
SG	Pass protect
ST	Pass protect
Q	Half roll for 3 steps and set, then drift to draw defense

Flavors of Laser

Red-Bus-Laser

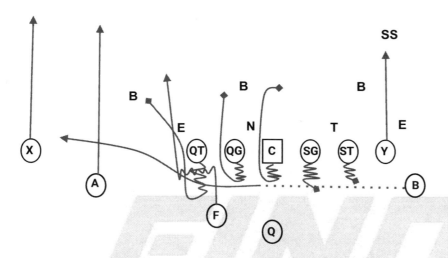

Practice

Practice

Scheme is important, but if the techniques are not taught correct, it will never matter. In order to maximize our time on drills it is important to organize practices. While I have an entire book available for those wanting to see how we organize practice, it is important to hit the general guidelines in this manual.

The main goals for us with our Offensive Line:
-Teach technique in Individual/Pod Time
       -Only work skills that lineman needs
-Work "timing" during Pre-Practice/Inside Time
-Work on game situations during Team Time

You will also see our "POD" time came about for us to focus on using drills that specific lineman needed. We work pulls only with linemen that need to pull.

"Inches make champions." - Vince Lombardi

How to Lose

One of the best things we have taught our linemen is teaching them to what is the most important part of their job for each play/concept. We want them to know what MUST be done each play and teach them some concepts or "tools" that will allow them to succeed. While we want to physically dominate our opponent, there are times that is not physically possible, so we must teach our linemen "how they can lose".

Some simple ways we teach this –

On down-blocks we want to encourage the defense up-field and then seal them down.

If we see a team that is great with hands and playing down the line. We will work to step to the up-field hip.

We don't ask for vertical push on must plays, we are much more interested in creating gaps.

Practice

Practice

In this next section I am going to walk through a variety of my practice plans. Some are from my time at a 4A school with most players going both ways and some will be from my time at a 6A school where players were able to only play one side of the ball. The first one is during a time when I was practicing our Senior and Junior High together to install our offense and defense with the Varsity coaches.

Each period is 5 minutes.

Some of the terminology is not the same.

I have included our defensive practice.

The top of the practice will show each position we are using. Some years we had enough coaches to cover these positions and some years we did not – you will notice that when you see how we "grouped" them to continue to get the drills in.

"We have a lot of mistakes in every practice. That's where we're at – correcting them and trying to improve the next day." – Bill Bellichick

Practice

This is a practice early in the season as we were working to install our offense and defense using varsity and junior high coaches together. Very good plan for those coaching 7-12 or installing the offense.

You will notice we ran the same drills with our groups and simply rotated senior high on offense and then defense.

In our group period we worked circuits this week. Working our "POD" system on the offensive line will come later or during a "blocking circuit".

We would split for team time at the end of practice. So that it was always varsity kids against varsity kids.

Time	PD	QB	F and B	Y	X and A	OL	DL	ILB	OLB	DB
	1	Senior High Special Teams				Junior High Tackling				
	2									
	3	Senior High Blocking Circuit				Junior High Special Teams				
	4									
	5	BREAK PERIOD								
	6	FTWK	FTWK	W/ OL		Indy	Jh:Off ball	JH: Agilities		JH: FTWK
	7	Tracks	Tracks	W/ OL		Indy	Jh: Stunts	JH: Horse	JH: 3 F's	JH: Ball
	8	Routes	Ball Drill	W/ WR	Routes	Indy	Jh: Read	JH: Keys	JH: Keys	JH: KEYS
	9	JH: FTWK	JH: FTWK	JH: W/ OL		JH: INDY	Off Ball	Agilities		FTWK
	10	JH: Tracks	JH: Tracks	JH: W/ OL		JH: INDY	Stunts	Horseshoe	3 F's	BALL
	11	JH: Routes	JH: Ball Dr	JH: W/ WR	JH: Routes	JH: INDY	Read	Keys	Keys	KEYS
	12	BREAK PERIOD								
	13	GROUP PERIOD: ROTATE DAYS								
	14	JH: Defensive Hip Drill / DL on Sled				SH: Blocking Circuit with OL / Skill working series				
	15	BREAK PERIOD								
	16	GROUP PERIOD: JH:								
	17									
	18	BREAK PERIOD								
	19	JH: OFFENSIVE TEAM				SH: DEFENSIVE TEAM				
	20									
	21									
	22	SH: OFFENSIVE TEAM				JH: DEFENSIVE TEAM				
	23									
	24									

Practice

This is a template for those coaches that don't have one-way players, but are attempting to get to one-way.

Notice periods 5-6 are for "crossover" players. So those guys that play the majority of the time one side of the ball can get a little bit of time on the other side of the ball. We have also started "cross training" offensive linemen in different positions during this period to build depth.

We also are working in periods 13-14 and 17-18 a time where are two-way players can get some additional time on both sides of the ball.

Also notice OL is getting time in periods 1-2.

PD	QB	T	Y/B	X and A	OL	DL	ILB	OLB	DB	
1	SPECIALTY PERIOD --- DC with Non-specialty defensive players --- OL Coach with all linemen not involved									
2	Coach With Kicker, Coach With PAT Group, Coach With Punter/Snapper, Coach With Returnmen									
3	SPECIAL TEAMS GROUP - ROTATE THROUGH MAIN 4 -- Steal time for QB/OL -- Steal time for DL/ILB or DB/OLB									
4										
5										Crossover
6										
7	BREAK					BREAK				
8										Indy/Pod
9										
10										
11										
12	BREAK					BREAK				
13	1's on 1's - 5 minute offense vs. our defense, 5 minute offense working cards									1 on 1s
14										
15	1 on 1's PASS PERIOD					1 on 1's INSIDE PERIOD				
16										
17	BREAK PERIOD					DEFENSIVE PERSONELL GROUPINGS				Defense groupings
18	OFFENSIVE PERSONNELL OR SPECIALS					BREAK PERIOD				Offense groupings
19	Situational Offensive Period (TEAM)					Situational Defensive Period				Vs. Scout group
20										
21										
22	BREAK									
23	CONDITIONING									
24										63

Practice

This is a Monday Practice at a 4A school with multiple players going both ways.

Periods 1-2 we are trying to "steal time" again for linemen.

Periods 3-6: we are working game plan in run game (since most of our OL never play special teams)

Periods 8-9 – Review of opponent on the field and lining up our scout team for the week.

Periods 10-11 – "Specials" and Adjustments for the week

PD	QB	F and B	Y	X and A	OL	DL	ILB	OLB	DB
1	Snaps/QB's		Punters-Snappers		Returners	OL-DOWN BLOCKS		WR-Ball Drills	
2	Snaps/QB's				Returners	OL-DOWN BLOCKS		PUNT BLOCK	
3	Punt Team								
4	KO					OL -- Discuss Personell and alignment			
5	KOR					Koby with OL			
6	PUNT RETURN								
7	BREAK								
8	Offense -- Review of Stuttgart -- 10 minutes								
9									
10	New Install -- (B/Y switch, BOGO-B Special, HVY REV, Simpson Special, Bus Y Special								
11									
12	BREAK								
13	Review of Stuttgart -- 5 Minutes together with DL								
14									
15	DL/ILB INDY					Formation Review with DB/OLB			
16									

Practice

This is a typical mid-late season Tuesday practice for us. Notice at a larger school we are able to accomplish more in less time as this one is only 18 periods. Earlier in the season or when athletes must go both ways, we typically are closer to 24 periods. We also "stole" time in periods 1-2 for our linemen.

Period 6 is our "pod" time: working B/T/WR's together. Zebra was "zone"

Period 7 is also "pod" time: working counter while WR's are working Quick game concepts and "other linemen" are working double team drill.

Periods 8-12: All working concepts as a group. With Period 11 being another "pod" time.

Period 13-14 was inside drill.

PD	QB	T	Y/B	X and A	OL	DL	ILB	OLB	DB	
1	Specialty Period -			60 pre-practice						
2				catches						
3	Kickoff Team				OL - DBL TEAMS		QB- White	DEF - Box Fits		
4	XP/FG Team									
5	POPS	POPS	Buck	POPS	DOWN BLOCK	HEEL LINE	Tackling and fits		FTWK	Indy Offense
6	G's/Nick/T's- Buck		B- Zeb Insert	Blocking	BASE BLOCK	BLOCK REC	Blitzes with OLB/ILB		ROUTES	
7	Q/Y/B/T - Counter PERIOD			Quick game	DBL TEAMS	Stunts	Run Fits	Ball To	Tackle/Fit	Indy Defense/Cross Train
8	Zone PERIOD				ZEBRA PERIOD	Block REC	Block Dest	Ball Away	Ball Drills	
9	BREAK PERIOD					BREAK PERIOD				
10	TRADE/SHIFT PERIOD/NEW SETS-FORMATIONS					STEM PD	MUG/BLUFF	Blitzes	Alignment	Pod/Group Work
11	QB/T/QT/QG- Slow Screen		B/X/A - Crack Blocking		ST/Y/SG/C - Cut	PASS RUSH	Key QB (Pass	Routes	Route Recogn	Primary Spot
12	PA PASS PERIOD					Blitzes with ILB's		Trips - (WIDE TRIPS)		
13	7 on 7 - Defensive focus			Trips/DBLS		Inside drill- Offensive Focus				Good on Good
14				Empty						
15	BREAK PERIOD									
16	Team offense					Team Defense				3rd Down
17										Hash Work
18										Red Zone

Practice

This practice was a typical Wednesday Practice. It is very similar to Tuesday's practice (of course working other areas of our offense), but notice we are now working new situations during team periods – 3rd and mediums, short yardage/heavy and working red zone again.

Also, the bottom period is where we work on air some situational football. We work a two-minute drill, XP, Onside Kick, Radar (Personnel package) defense and then a "win the game" two-minute drill.

Offensive line we steal time in periods 1-4. We are also working our "counter POD" period 8.

PD	QB	T	Y/B	X and A	OL	DL	ILB	OLB	DB	
1	Specialty Period -			Pre-Practice	OL - Skip Pulls (G's and QT)			Def - Turnover/Fits		
2			Ball Security		OL - Cuts					
3	KOR				OL - HINGE		QB- White	DEF - Box Fits		
4	Kickoff		QB/WR - Quick Game		Defense - Turnover Period					
5	POPS	POPS	Buck	POPS	DOWN	HEEL LINE	KEYS	TACKLING - CIRCLE		INDY - OFFENSE
6	G's/T's/Q - Belly	B- 2nd Level	Now/Bub	BASE	READ BLCK	FITS FROM SPACE		MAVERICK		
7	Bus Passes	With OL	Y/OL	Flood/Snag	SPLITS CHEATS	Fire Off	KEYS/Fits	FORCE-FIT	ALIGN	INDY - DEFENSE
8	Counter Period - Y/G/T/B/Q			Crack Blocks	Cut/Hinge	DOWN LINE	Off Blocks	Off Blocks	ROUTES	
9	BREAK PERIOD					BREAK PERIOD				
10	FLEX PERIOD					STEMS	RUN FITS	Alignment and Route Recognitio		Pod/Group Work
11	MUSTANG PERIOD					Pass Rush	Drops-Key QB	Fits in run game		Primary Spot
12	PLAY ACTION / SCREEN PERIOD					BLITZ PERIOD FRONT 7			MAVERICK	
13	7 on 7 Period - Priority Defense			Trips/DBLS	Inside Run Period - Offense Priority (English)					
14				Empty						
15	BREAK PERIOD									
16	Team Offense 5 3rd and med, Spread Personnel, RED ZONE					Team Defense - Base, 2 PT Plays, Wildcat				Short Yardage
17										Specials / Heavy
18										Run Game
19	Play the game Situations on Air - 2 minute drive offense - finish with "fire" XP/FG, Onside Kick, RADAR DEFNSE, 2 min drive offense									
20										Short Yardage

Practice Segments

Practice

How to structure it in Practice

-Individual time: Coaches working drills against technique we will see in a game. We need to work "all situations" so that is on Wednesday during INDY time. Should be CONSTANT FEEDBACK FROM COACH.

-Group time: Working each run/pass concept vs. predicted front/coverages. On Wednesday we will work "other looks". This time needs to be faster pace, but still take time on feedback.

-Team: Work situations in each rep from the defense. We usually only work predicted front with 5-10 "inserts" each week in team.

All practices need to contain at least 3 elements

-Individual time: Working on specific skills and developing each player. For the Offensive Line this time is critical to development. Be sure these are drills that match needs for the game.

-Group time: Smaller groups (I will go in detail on how we use "PODS" and Inside/7 on 7 later) to work on timing.

-Team time: This is where each team must practice the situations of the game.

 # Individual Drills

Individual

The goal is to work "daily" drills that translate directly to Friday Night
-We want to prioritize the different areas for each position
-Spend the most time on areas that we use the most

We don't want "mindless reps" here, but we do want a high volume of reps

A coach should never "be done" with these drills as they are the foundation to what we do

Individual time should be "sacred" time for all position coaches. This is the time to address specific areas this position group struggled with or to work to highlight skill sets.

Generally, we will give 20-25 minutes a day here early in the season and cut it back to 10-15 minutes as the season progresses, but we are always looking for ways to "steal" time for these players.

Make a priority list on Sunday meetings for the week and then work those priorities in the form of drills throughout the week.

Better to get 10 quality reps that 100 mindless ones.

We often "steal" more time with our offensive line during pre-practice and special teams. This can be time for areas we struggle or scheme related issues.

 # Individual Time

Using Individual and Adjustments

Offensive line – Working the technique over the alignment (it changes often for us)

    -Monday/Tuesday/Thursday – Predicted front/technique

    -Wednesday – Other front/techniques/Blitzes to be prepared

This is how we structure our offensive line time during the season. We want to make sure we are working expected fronts/coverages for 3 of the 4 days that week and then working a "worst case scenario".

This needs to be done in individual time as we may not have much time during team/inside drill to hit multiple looks.

Many time's our Offensive Line Coach will cover these during Pre-Practice or Specialty Time.

"Pod" work

PODS

This is to work areas of our offense that need to work together
- Guards and Skill players on run game
- WR's and QT on screen game
- QB and OL – on runs/blitz pickup
- Wingback/TE with OL Coach
- Wingback with WR Coach

*The goal here is to put coach with expertise coaching the skill --

This is the area we separate our system from most others. I believe the POD system we have started is one of the best things we do in practice. This allows us to maximize time, reps and handle more players with less coaches.

It also allows coaches to work with different players which leads to better team cohesion.

In the next pages I will go through a few different set ups we use. I would encourage each of you to work to come up with your own "PODS" that work for your athletes.

"Pod" work

This is the first type of POD we use when we are working Buck Sweep.

Guards and QB/RB together in the middle.

OL – Working down blocks in left corner

Y/B – Working scenarios on down block in right corner

WR's – Working screen/quick game/blocking at bottom

5 minute period with a lot of reps. We will change up the QB read each time.

"Pod" work

Here is another view of this set up. I go into detail later in the drill section, but this "POD" of players would be working while the other positions are working on the skills they need.

Notice we will use moveable, inexpensive equipment if possible so that we can quickly set up and move each practice. We work POD's as much as possible since they allow us to work on specific skills needed.

"Pod" work

This is a close-up of our POD drill time for buck sweep. Notice we have a line coach, RB coach and QB coach all involved in this POD. At this school I was blessed to have multiple coaches working the offensive side of the ball.

At other schools, this POD has been run by one coach due to not having as many coaches available.

I go through this more in-depth in the drill portion of this manual.

"Pod" work

This POD is our "Belly" POD.

We are working guards on wrap blocking with QB/RB.

At the bottom we have our WR/B working blocking in space for screens.

At the top right we have our other linemen working double teams.

"Pod" work

Another view of our POD work. We will often work this inside of our "RPO" read. During this time the rest of our line will be working base blocking or double teams that marry-with "Belly".

"Pod" work

This POD is our slow screen POD.

We are working slow screens with our QT/QG and RB/QB.

At the top our other linemen are working pass pro.

At the bottom you can see our WR/B working crack blocking.

 # Inside-RPO

The next section of our practice is our "Inside" period. During this time, we often will pair up a quick game period.

For instance, all the line, B, F and QB will be working run game. On the other end of the field our X/A (and sometimes B) will be working screen/quick game.

This period is generally on Tuesday/Wednesday for 10 minutes and we want to be sure to hit all our base runs. We want high tempo and to record this period.

Here is an example of 2019. Right off the picture to the left is our WR coach working with our X/A. The rest of our offense is working inside drill and our "steal" RPO for the QB.

 # Team

In my opinion this is the area of practices most coaches begin to lose their athletes. If done correctly, each athlete has already worked on the skills and this time should be a "game-like" scenario.

To help this happen I script situations for every snap during team. From hash work to 3rd downs to red zone to time management. We want to cover all of these as we are getting "reps" with our plays.

Early in the season I'd recommend doing this by "series". Or working buck series, belly series, etc... As you get closer to the season and during in-season practices it is always best to work plays as you'd call them in a game. So, working "situational football" is the best way to run your team sessions of practice.

On the next page I go through how I have chosen to break it down. This will insure as a coach you (AND YOUR PLAYERS) understand what plays you plan to call for every situation. Knowing as a coach is great, but having your team know and feel confident is the key.

Team

16	Team offense				Team Defense			3rd Down
17								Hash Work
18								Red Zone

16	Team Offense	5 3rd and med, Spread Personnel, RED ZONE			Team Defense - Base, 2 PT Plays, Wildcat			Short Yardage
17								Specials / Heavy
18								Run Game
19	Play the game Situations on Air - 2 minute drive offense - finish with "fire" XP/FG, Onside Kick, RADAR DEFNSE, 2 min drive offense							
20								Short Yardage

Here are a few examples of how we do "team" above.

Remember to organize each day to hit all situations you will face in a game. Below are what I'd recommend.

Practicing Structure

Structure your days of the week so that you can get each situation you may face – Here is what we do on offense and defense each day:

Monday – Base plays, adjustments, game plan adjustments, 3rd/4th and shorts, installs

Tuesday – Hash work, Red zone work, 3rd and longs, 2 Minute drill

Wednesday – Short yardage, Gimmicks, Special Formations, 4 Minute drill
*Other defensive looks in individual and pod time (not in team)

Thursday – Review all situations and hit all (time scenarios)

Drills

"Knowledge is confidence. And confidence lets you play fast." – Bill Parcells

Drills

When we begin to build our drills for the offensive line, we start with a priority list. It is easy to spend massive amounts of time on drills that may not really translate to what they need to accomplish. To this end we have some drills that every lineman must go through and we will work these everyday. You will find many of these drills in this section.

However, we also have a few drills that are specifically for our guards and tight ends since they are the only ones we ask to pull in our offense. Those drills we attempt to always accomplish in our "POD" time. When we build a practice, we start with drills each lineman needs to do.

We then work on drills that are the most important for us that season. Since we know Buck and Counter will be in our playbook each season, we work **down blocks** very often. If we are going to run a lot of Belly, we will be sure to work our **base blocks** and **double team blocks**. If we feel we will be a heavy screen team, we will work **spatial blocking** and so-on.

Basically, be sure to prioritize these drills to match the plays you feel will be you most important plays in a given season and adjust as you go.

Drills

Another way we build our drill book is through plays. For example, these are the drills that help often with Buck and Counter. We must be able to Down Block and Pull.

When we go to our "POD" time we will split the linemen into groups so that they can work on each portion of this blocking scheme. The guards on pulling and the rest of the line on down blocking.

DOWN BLOCK DRILL	2ND LEVEL DRILL
TURN BACK TO HOLE	B B
DL DL DL	
COACH	COACH
HURDLE	
Q F	
COACH	

Drills

These are our top drills we will run with our line each year. In each drill you will find:

1) Purpose and Skill we are working on
2) Set up of the drill
3) Coaching points to give
4) Common mistakes to avoid

I have also labeled which linemen (from all to "guards") need to be working a drill. We want to make sure that we are working the drills that matter and spending the most time on the most important drills.

Each season, coaches will adapt their play-calling, but I have ordered the most common way we would prioritize our drills in this section.

"There are no shortcuts to building a team each season. You build the foundation brick by brick." – Bill Belichick

E.D.D.

These are our "EDD" or Every-Day Drills. We want to get these in every day in the spring/summer and at least on 2-3 days each week. Often, we will build these drills into our "warm-up" period.

These are drills that every lineman and our "Y" need to get often. They are not position specific, but drills for every spot on the line. We will work these the first day we begin working "football" and continue though the last week we play.

The biggest challenge in these drills is to not become "bored" but to focus on why they are important. Work hard to make sure your athletes understand why they need these drills.

HANDS/CORE DRILL

ALL LINEMEN

PURPOSE

To teach our keeping our hands inside and maintaining balance.

Good warm up drill

I want to acknowledge this is from "Tip of the Spear" as a good drill for leverage.

DRILL INSTRUCTIONS

Players will partner-up and put hands as if the are praying.

The partner will push and try to knock them off-balance

KEY SKILLS

Balanced Stance
Hnads inside
Core and arm strength

SETUP

Done in partners

COMMON MISTAKES

Players lean to contact instead of keep balance

Base is to narrow

COACHING POINTS

Good warm up drill or drill to teach hands inside and balance.

STANCE DRILL

ALL LINEMEN

PURPOSE

To teach our line balance in their stances. We will adjust based on personnel, but want to teach a few key components.

KEY SKILLS

Balanced Stance
Ability to block down or pull
Weight Distrribution

SETUP

Can be done with a chute
Can be done with hurdles
Can be done with partners

DRILL INSTRUCTIONS

Coaches will stand behind the players and use partners (if no chute is available) to work on keeping their shoulders down. We want to work on a forward bend with little weight on our hands. Would like feet shoulder width to slightly wider. We teach our inside hands down.

COMMON MISTAKES

Feet too wide
Weight too far forward
Bending at waist, but not at knees

COACHING POINTS

Start with leanding forward in a 2 point stance and then let the hand drag the ground. In the bottom picture we probably have too much weight forward.

PLUS DRILL

ALL LINEMEN

PURPOSE

First step
We are working on staying low coming out of our stance
6 inch step

KEY SKILLS

Weight stays centered
Short step
STAY LOW

SETUP

Preferably on an "X" on the field

Need a line

Chute or Partners

DRILL INSTRUCTIONS

We will set up on an "X" if possible to highlight the step. If we are working with a large group we want them on a line.

If done with partners we want to make the goal to stay low.

6 inch step on a down block is main goal..

COMMON MISTAKES

Too big a step
Raise up
Lean forward too much .

COACHING POINTS

Work on keeping the "bend in the knees"

Stay low by bending, not lunging

Short step to keep balance

DOWN BLOCK
ALL LINEMEN

PURPOSE

Teaching how to block down on a first level defender

DRILL INSTRUCTIONS

We like to do this with partner set up and in increments of steps.

Plus drill and then we add step 2 and then future steps

We want to step and get head to the hip of the defender and use outside hand to keep them inside.

COMMON MISTAKES

Stepping upfield too far

Too large steps

Not bringing outside hand to drive defenders.

COACHING POINTS

We teach 2 types of defenders (folowing pages) and that will adjust aiming point, but early on we focus on upfield teams.

6 inch steps and turn body in a 180 by end of the drill..

KEY SKILLS

Maintaining balance

Working the defender down and keeping body between them an ball carrier

SETUP

Done with partners that will off-set to be "down" for our linemen.

Use hands to encourage low pad level

DOWN BLOCK DRILL

TURN BACK TO HOLE

COACH

 # Down Block

Down Block for "Heel Line" Defenders

We struggled very much with "over the top" players on Buck/Outside runs

This drill will force OL/TE/Wing to work hips to sideline

We call it "over the top" --- Goal is for all down blockers to end up with their butt to the endzone we are working towards

Down Block

Down Block for "Up-field" Defenders

When playing a team that relies on penetration, we will work flatter steps in this drill and stress getting our head across the defender.

We will often have the "defenders" (players) step forward at the snap to change the angle for our down block.

Down Block

Down Block – B/Y combo

Another part of the down block circuit we will add is working our B in at an angle. We can do this on his own or we will work him in tandem with our TE since they are the key to blocking for buck sweep.

We will simply move our coach to different techniques to simulate the defense and have them both work on down blocks and on communication.

ALL LINEMEN

PURPOSE

Teaching Down Blocks on LB/DB players at the 2nd level of the defense. This has been very diffficult for our linemen as they want to "chase" defensive players..

KEY SKILLS

Learning to block an area and not chase a man.

Coming to "balance" to block a skilled defender.

SETUP

Partners back up 5 yards and 2-3 yards inside.

Coach gives direction to "stay" or work over the top to the "defense".

DRILL INSTRUCTIONS

We set up a partner line 5 yards deep. The coach will tell them on the "snap" if they remain in place or run to the outside (the reactions we see in a game).

Linemen will block the man down or if he leaves they stay on the path an block the next partner..

COMMON MISTAKES

Linemen chase their partner

The angle they take is too flat

Don't settle their feet to block.

COACHING POINTS

This is a spacial type of block so we must gather our balance and use our hands and leverage.

Don't chase the LB if he flys over the top.

2ND LEVEL DRILL

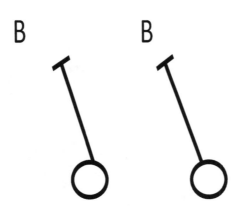

B   B

COACH

Down Block

Down blocking on the second level is much more about understanding leverage of the defense. This is an example of our wing blocking down on an inside linebacker. Notice he steps flat to the block, if the LB shoots he is ready.

Once he identifies the LB is playing over the top he repositions to his back hip to seal him inside. This run resulted in a touchdown, due to this block and seal.

PULL KICK

POSITION: Guards and Tightends

PURPOSE

Teaching our linemen to kick a force player

Used with buck/counter

DRILL INSTRUCTIONS

We will usually work this with hurdles to create an obvious target

We want our linemen to "pull the lawn mower" and get 3 depth steps and then move TOWARDS THE LINE as they kick the force player.

COMMON MISTAKES

Linemen are not tight enough to the line and allow force player inside.

Don't get depth on first 3 steps

Slow down on contact.

COACHING POINTS

Hit with same shoulder in direction you ar pulling – Pull Right, Hit Right

Run through the block

Come "downhill" to create a great angle.

Do not slow down – force defender to run upfield.

KEY SKILLS

Teaching leverage on kicks

Speed and footwrk

Angles of the pull

SETUP

We prefer oversized hurdles, but can use bags or cones.

Want to do this on a line.

At times we will cone off the area to force depth on first 3 steps.

Pull Kick

The kick-out block is key in buck sweep in our offense and in counter and power in most other offenses. This is a clear example of coming down-hill and attacking the correct shoulder. Look at the gap that is created as we "pull left, hit left" on this kick. The gap will be widened as we run through the defender.

We want to strike quickly and with the correct leverage. We are fine if we "miss" as long as the defender works up-field. The next page will show what to do after contact.

Pull Kick

Here is the next clip of the same block. The defender is sealed out and he cannot escape inside. The goal of our kick out is to create a seal and not allow him back over our inside shoulder. Once contact is made, we want to push him up-field as shown in this picture. Notice the guard has his hand on the back hip of the force player and is escorting him up-field and out of the play.

The defender can run as far up-field as possible, we simply do not want him to cross our face and get into the hole we have now created.

PULL LOG
POSITION: Guards and

FIND WAY

PURPOSE

Teaching our linemen to Log a force player

Used with buck/counter

DRILL INSTRUCTIONS

Learning when to log (seal) a player

Coach/Scout player will step very flat down the line – DO NOT GET UPFIELD

Pulling linemen will run to same spot as kick, but when he doesn't have the angle will work to seal – run his feet and force inside.

Common Mistakes

Linemen will anticipate the log and run deeper than normal.

Feet will stop on contact and no seal is ever made

COACHING POINTS

We want to kick everything, so run to kick and react to log.

Once the kick has failed, run feet in a circle to seal the defender inside.

KEY SKILLS

Teaching leverage

Understand how to read defensive player

How to "seal" a crashing defensive player

SETUP

We want to run this with a coach if possible so they can see how and when to log a player.

Coach will step flat and not allow space for a kick.

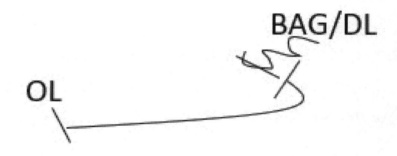

Pull Log

We do not often log, but here is an example of the same guard that was kicking a defender working his feet to seal the player.

When we identify the need to log, we want to work our feet in almost a circle and seal the defensive player inside. This is using their technique against them and is often more of a technical block.

We want to make sure this block is only used when a kick is not going to happen. Often pullers will try to do this too often since it seems easier, but it will string the play out.

PULL WRAP

POSITION: Guards and Tightends

PURPOSE

Teaching our pullers to stay on their track and not chase defensive players.

KEY SKILLS

Getting depth on pull

Getting squared to the line

Eyes inside

Staying on path

SETUP

Working with 2 "LB's" set up

Coach will signal where the linebackers will fit

Wrapping player will pick up whichever LB steps to his gap

DRILL INSTRUCTIONS

We want to use this as a way to enforce staying on our path

We will use cones to enforce depth and bags/hurdles to work on setting path, but we want bodies to create a read for our OL as they wrap.

COMMON MISTAKES

Not enough depth on pull

Do not get square to line

Chasing LB instead of running path

COACHING POINTS

Get depth to get out of trash.

Take first daylight and keep eyes inside

Run your path – don't chase

Run through contact – do not slow down

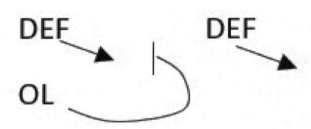

Pull Wrap

Great example of a pull wrap, as we can see the guard had created depth on his pull. He is not square to the line of scrimmage with his eyes searching inside for the linebacker/safety that will fit.

Notice he is leaning forward and is running at close to full speed as we want this to hit as quickly as possible. Remember, the running back will make him right if a defender wants to dance.

BASE BLOCK

POSITION

PURPOSE

Working on pad level and hand placement as we drive a defender.

We will work straight ahead early, but really focus on moving them horizontially.

KEY SKILLS

Keep feet moving

Fit hands inside of pads

If we are working angle, force defender and seal them and then drive

SETUP

Done with partners

Can use bags early

Can use rubber "boards" to keep feet separated.

DRILL INSTRUCTIONS

We are working our "base" block. Taking a defensive player either back or blocking them out in our offense.

Limenen come out of stance and drive feet – wide base and tight hands through the whistle.

COMMON MISTAKES

Stopping feet or taking long steps

Feet get too narrow

Grabbing outside of defenders

Raising up too quickly

COACHING POINTS

Short choppy steps

Shoulder width base

Keep hands inside

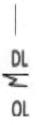

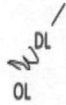

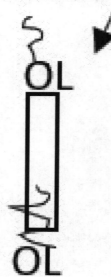

 # Base Block

We are not perfect on this base block, but are doing a lot of things correctly. The tackle has positioned his body to protect the hole and drive the defender out but stepping with his inside foot. He has also done a great job of keeping his hands inside of the defensive player. Finally, he is winning the leverage battle by keeping his pads lower and has good bend in his knees to drive.

REACH BLOCK
All Linemen

PURPOSE

Teaching Reach Blocks

We use these on Jet and a similar block on Roll-out passing..

DRILL INSTRUCTIONS

We set up in partners and ask our "Defensive Linemen" to fight upfield or outside.

When we begin this process we start in a 2-PT stance.

We will progress it to our stance and work on getting our inside hand through the outside shoulder of the DL..

COMMON MISTAKES

Feet Stop

Grabbing cloth on shoulder of DL – That will be called holding

.

COACHING POINTS

We want to work to get our inside hand through the outside of the defensive player.

Run your feet.

Do not grab.

KEY SKILLS

Teaching to Reach outside shoulder of the DL.

SETUP

This is easiest to do with partners.

Can make this easier by starting in a 2-PT stance and cheating leverage.

Progress up to stance and wide techniques. .

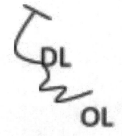

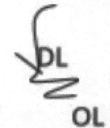

We will combine this with all our offensive line to work on coming off to 2nd level and staying on our track.

If we "cannot" reach the DL then we will base him out and drive him upfield as far as possble for our running back to cut back.

 # Reach Block

Out goal on a reach block is to get our inside hand through the defenders outside shoulder before starting to turn. This is a great example by our tackle of using his feet to get into a great position. The next part of the block would be to engage with both hands and seal the defender and drive him back.

CUT DRILL
ALL LINEMEN

PURPOSE

Working the cut block on inside defenders.

We want to stress not simply diving.

KEY SKILLS

Going low and rolling through contact.

Keep head out of contact and learn to aim where the defensive linemen is moving toward.

SETUP

Best to use with larger dummies

Partners will off-set inside

Coach stands behind OL to watch/critique

DRILL INSTRUCTIONS

We will work partners holding bags. OL will shoot through the bag and bear-crawl and/or roll through contact.

Partners then switch.

COMMON MISTAKES

Diving in wrong angle

Simply "belly flopping"

Leading with head

COACHING POINTS

Aim flatter than you want

Roll through contact

Narrow stance

PURPOSE

Working on Picking up blitzers in pass protection.

We teach a vertical set, protecting inside gap first and passing off to outside.

KEY SKILLS

Balance

Communication

Footwork

SETUP

Run with partnered groups of 2.

Coach will stand behind and direct stunts and areas he wants the scout defense to move.

DRILL INSTRUCTIONS

We will attempt to do this drill with partners and two scout players to simulate 2nd level pass rush.

The coach stands behind and tells the stunt to the scout players.

OL will pass set and communicate the stunt while protecting the inside.

COMMON MISTAKES

Linemen will lunge at defenders instead of maintain balance.

No communication on Blitzing.

Turn shoulders out and allow inside rush.

COACHING POINTS

Keep Shoulders Square

Communicate

Punch first level defender, but keep eyes on second level defender

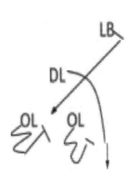 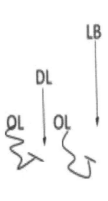

We will also work this and not blitz the LB.

Or we can work this with 2 DL that will twist.

The goal is force communication and balance with our offensive line.

 # POD DRILLS

These are drills that need to be worked with and for specific spots on our line. It is a skill that a specific position in our offense needs to be able to execute. While it would not be "wrong" to do this with all linemen, it would be wasted time as we never as those positions to perform these blocks.

In this section you will find POD's for our guards, quick side of the line, center/guards, guards/tackles, guards and tight-ends and more. We basically want to work positions that will perform these types of blocks together.

This would include:
Double Team Drills – While we rep these with all players, we want to focus on those who work together.

Pull Drills – Often our Guards and Tight-ends.

Screen Drills – One side of the line or the middle of the line.

HURDLE DRILL
Guards and Y's

PURPOSE

Working on blocking on pulls.

This is used in Buck, Belly and Counter.

DRILL INSTRUCTIONS

We will move the hurdles to simulate kickout blocks and wrap blocks. This drill will be used in mutliple ways.

The goal is to work footwork for pulling.

Often we will include our backfield action.

COMMON MISTAKES

Slowing down at hurdle

Not running as fast as possible.

COACHING POINTS

We want to run "through the block" so we use the hurdles.

Angle the hurdles to cause the wrapping guard to get his "eyes inside".

We will often move the kick hurdle up-field to simulate coming "downhill" on kick blocks.

KEY SKILLS

Learning angles and how to explode through blocks.

We want the wrapping guard to gain depth on his 2-4th steps and then square to the line.

HURDLE

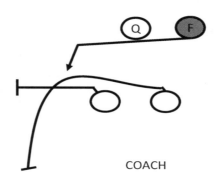

COACH

SETUP

We like oversized Hurdles, but this drill can be done with cones/dummies.

Hurdle Drill

A picture of our "Hurdle" drill. We will often add in hurdles for our linemen to work on coming out of their stance low. Notice in this picture the 4' hurdle that is next to our Quick Guard to cause him to come out of his stance low.

We also will angle the hurdles slightly to cause our linemen to run at the correct angle. The "kick" hurdle is angled out to cause our guard to work on "rooting out" the defensive player and the "pull" hurdle is angled inside to cause our guard to get his eyes and body angled to pick up an inside player.

Hurdle Drill

The next progression from the hurdle drill is to remove the hurdles. Now we will use coaches or scout players to represent the defense.

We do this to get more of a moving target and game-like look for our guards. They run through the correct hip of the coach and we can simulate pressure from different areas.

Hurdle Drill

This is the goal for our wrapping guard. Notice how he has his eyes "inside" looking for pursuit. He will naturally want to "chase" defenders and we do not want this. We want him to run his track and the running back will cut off of him. We also NEVER WANT TO SLOW DOWN. This is why we use the hurdles and progress up.

Quick Side of Line and Center

PURPOSE

Working blocks for screen game or 2nd level down blocks. Blocks that require us to "come to balance".

DRILL INSTRUCTIONS

We will begin with cones and progress to people.

We want linemen to work to release down field and settle at a "hip" of the player.

The "hip" represents the leverage we want them to keep.

COMMON MISTAKES

Do not come to balance

Work at wrong angles – go where the defense will be not where they are.

.

COACHING POINTS

We will set this drill up in multiple ways to simulate plays/blocks.

The main point is to get feet moving and come to balance.

KEY SKILLS

Quick Feet

Great Balance

SETUP

In the set-up below we have a screen drill.

We will also do this with downblocking at the 2nd level.

Often we will take the quick tackle and only work him with the WR's on screen drills.

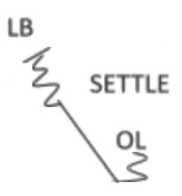

 # Blocking in Space

Blocking in space is key for most of our linemen (with the main exception being our Strong Tackle. We do work different types of blocking in space depending on the position.

The main screens we run are to the quick side or middle of the field. So, we often work our Quick Side of the line, with a coach/cones as this block does require them to settle in space. We will also work with our interior linemen for our middle screen.

While we are working this drill, we are often working the other linemen on pass protection or a block they need improvement on.

 # **Blocking in Space**

Blocking in space is difficult for linemen. We usually take them with our WR's or at least our WR coach to teach them how to understand angles and how to settle our feet.

In this picture #3 is doing a great job of coming to balance and will take the defender wherever he chooses to go on this fast screen. #22 is working his leverage on the linebacker and forcing him to commit to coming under or over the block and then he will engage.

Most of the work on blocking in space is effort and coming to balance for our linemen. Allowing them to work with a coach that understands that will help tremendously.

Counter POD Drill
SG and Y

PURPOSE

Working TE/G's on pull kick and wrap drill for our Counter Play.

Can be used for other pull drills.

KEY SKILLS

Working on angle of kick and the angle of the wrap.

We want to gain depth with TE as he pulls to wrap.

SETUP

Often done with our over-sized hudles or with coaches/bags.

Done on a line to work depth of pulls.

DRILL INSTRUCTIONS

We like to do this with the backfield action so we can work angles and timing for counter.

Will often use hurdles/dummies early in the season to give angles.

COMMON MISTAKES

Pull Kick – slows down or takes on with wrong shoulder

Pull Wrap – does not get enough depth on pull or get his eyes back inside.

COACHING POINTS

We want to "rip the lanwmower" as we pull.

TE should gain depth on steps 2-4 and then get square. He almost runs a "U" shape to get his eyes inside.

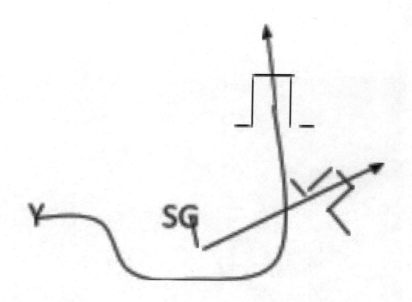

 # POD for Counter

This drill is common for us to start off with using the hurdles we do on our Buck Drill. As we progress, we like to have coaches/scout players representing defenders. We teach this the same as our buck sweep drill.

This drill was on a Thursday practice before we started our quick practice, thus no hurdles or coaches.

We will rotate through all of our guards and tight-ends as well as the backfield portion.

DOUBLE TEAM
ALL LINEMEN

PURPOSE

Working on coming off to LB

We want to teach how to communicate as we work to 2nd level.

DRILL INSTRUCTIONS

The goal is to give multiple looks in this drill.

We will move our DL from a shade, to head up.

Also, want our LB to fit over the top or fit inside.

COMMON MISTAKES

Both linemen leave DL and do not get push.

OL does not see second level defenders and drop their head..

COACHING POINTS

We want to have our hands and no space between our OL.

We want to "Post and knock".

One Linemen gets vertical push and the other wants to knock him and seal him horizontally.

KEY SKILLS

Keeping contact 1st level defenders.

We want to post and knock

Usually our inside player will "post" with his outside hand and keep eyes on LB

Our knock player will "knock" them inside with his shoulder as he keeps his eyes on the 2nd level defender.

SETUP

We will use a scout player at the first level and another playing at LB depth.

Coach will point to where he wants the LB to "fit".

We will also move our DL in other places.

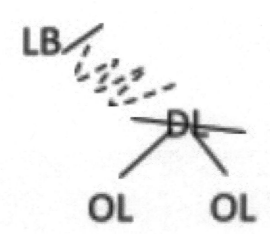

118

Opponent Prep

Opponent Prep

My goal when scouting opponents is to ensure that we focus mostly on the ability level of the opponent. With this offense we will see multiple looks that are not the same as they would show against a "10 personnel" team or "normal offense". So while we do work predicted alignment we are more concerned with the following:

1) Studs and Duds – in the box and in the secondary
2) Technique of the DL/ILB – Squeeze and pinch or up-field disrupters
3) Keys oriented or blitz/movement oriented

We will also look over as much film as possible to see what their potential adjustments are to a TE/Wing look. Often you may see similar looks and be able to make an educated guess as to what the defense will do.

Opponent Prep

Scouting Opponents for Offense
Offensive line – Are they pressure team or technique? Any tells in stance to blitzes or stunts?

This is what we want our athletes to know. I want my coaches to know much more about our opponent, but we want to be very careful with how much we give our athletes.

We want our team to work all week on the technique they will see. We see plenty of different alignments each week, but the techniques of the defensive players cannot be changed in a week. If we know their theory and style of play, we can work to prepare.

This list is the minimum I want my athletes to know. If they can handle more information, we want them to have it.

Example – If we have an experienced lineman, we trust we will allow him to make adjustment calls in game.

Alignment

Alignment

One of the concepts we have attempted to work with our linemen on is how to give them an advantage pre-snap. This can be accomplished by moving their splits or depth.

In our base alignment we teach –

1) 2 Ft splits
2) Guards, Tackles and TE headgear on center's hips
3) Wing can touch the TE's hip and is equal width and depth away (generally 2 x 2)

In this next section I will show a few pictures of our alignment and some "cheats" we use to help on specific plays. The bottom line is attempting to give your linemen as much advantage as possible before the snap.

Also, teach them "how to lose". Where it is OK to get beat. We want to mash people and be very physical, but the reality in some seasons is that we are over-matched physically. If they understand how to use influence and other tools to take the Defensive Line in the direction we want, we consider that a win.

 # Shifts-Cheats

Using motions and shifts has become something many offenses are starting to use. I highly recommend using them to "spice" up or give your offense an advantage. Here are a few simple ones:

1) Linemen splits – Teach your line to cheat splits on Belly or any gap play to create larger natural gaps. Also, teach them to cheat closer for double teams. This may sound basic, but it has really helped our offensive line.

2) Use motion more often against man-to-man teams. Those teams will kill your RPO game, but you can make up for it by shifting and quick motioning.

3) Quick huddle – I don't talk a lot about quick huddling, but if you want to gain an advantage huddling 2 yards off the ball with your line and then getting on the ball and snapping it quickly will make it difficult for the defense to adapt.

4) Using "over" sets where your tight end lines up weak will also cause issues with a defense identifying strength if you do them quickly and can create and uncovered player.

Stance

Our base stance is slightly wider that shoulder-width apart with our feet and our toe about 6 inches back from our front foot. We do want a forward lean, but do not want much (if any) weight on our front hand.

We would like a flat-back, but as you can see in this picture we do not look perfectly uniform, we will adjust to our athletes each season.

Typical issues you will need to fix:
1) No bend in knees
2) Too much weight forward and no balance
3) Too wide – the last player in this picture is almost too wide for how we would like their stance.
4) Too big of a stagger in depth of feet

Stance

This is how we teach our Wingback's to align early in the season. Notice he is reaching to check on depth by touching the Tight End.

We have rotated from an angled stance (like in this picture) to a squared stance (you will see in another picture) each season.

If we feel we have athletic wings that need help blocking, we will angle them. If we feel they are good at blocking, but need help getting into space we square them up.

Alignment - Cheats

Here is our base alignment with our full line and wing back. We have a few cheats we will do based on personnel and plays (later in this section and in the IF-THEN section).

Notice each lineman has their outside and down in their stance and the stances do not look exactly the same as each other since we have different athletes.

Cheats

Over the past few seasons, we have started moving our alignment around to benefit our player or for a specific play. While I will go through the player adjustments in the IF-THEN section, here are a few cheats we like for play selection or against specific looks.

On this play we are running a strong side run – buck sweep.

We have cheated our Quick Tackle very wide to take the 5 technique as far as he would go.

We have also cheated our Strong Tackle in to make the block on the 2 technique and cheated our Quick Guard in to help the center back block on the 2 technique.

Cheats

On this play we are running a strong side run – belly.

We have cheated our Quick Tackle very wide to take the 5 technique as far as he would go.

We have also cheated our Strong Tackle and Strong Guard's splits to they can double team the 2 technique to backside LB.

We have also cheated our Quick Guard in to help the center back block on the 2 technique.

As we progress, we will also widen our TE splits on the 9 technique.

Cheats

Other plays we can run splits to help:

On Buck we tend to squeeze our splits more often to help with down-blocking.

On Counter we will take our QT as wide as the DE will allow.

On Belly we will teach our TE to cheat his alignment.

In order to do this, you must make sure your Linemen know the concepts of the play and how they can "get beat" and also how the must never "get beat". This will allow them to often do this on their own during a game.

Often, we will refer to these as "smart splits". Or understanding how to make our job easier by alignment.

If – Then

Built in Answers

If-Then

One of the reasons this offense was developed was the premise of the Wing T – IF the defense does this, THEN the offense should do this…

This premise was also big in the RPO game – that is the reason it was invented – to place players in conflict. IF the defender does this, THEN the offense runs/passes.

In any offense this should be the thought process. Have built in adjustments ready to go. This offense was designed to have these built in to any play concept we install. Having these available should provide answers for whatever the defense throws at you.

In this section I plan to go over 5 of the main "IF-THEN" questions I get asked about with this offense.

If-Then

IF we have a lineman that struggles with speed…

THEN

1) Work to narrow his stance

2) Cheat his splits in and those around him in on all down blocks/double teams

3) Cheat his splits out on all "base" blocks if you have a "Shaded defender"

4) If you only have one, I'd play him at Strong Tackle and never ask him to free release to 2nd level. Always a Gap-Down player and you will need to RPO 2nd level players or double team to them.

If-Then

IF we are undersized up front…

THEN

1) Work on as wide of splits as possible if you are quick.

2) Work to have flat-backed stances and low pad level.

3) Cut often

4) Teach "base" blocks as more of a "seal" not a drive block.

If-Then

IF we see a penetrating/blitzing front

THEN

1) Cut the splits of the offensive linemen down

2) Run Belly series more and try to get double teams

3) Screen game should be available

4) Roll QB out in the passing game with jet motion

5) Hard count or quick count to slow down the defensive line

If-Then

IF we see a defense that is great at reading keys and playing technique…

THEN

1) Work on wider splits and stepping more up-field on all first steps to seal off Defensive Linemen.

2) Use some "influence" blocking schemes – Down block to get them to collapse, Pull Guards opposite, etc…

3) Run more RPO game.

4) Give run reads with pulls in same direction as the play and run "naked" boots/counters.

If-Then

IF we are not able to get movement against a 9 Technique

THEN

1) Run "bypass" and kick him out if he is an up-field penetrating defensive player.

2) Have the TE base him for 1-count before releasing inside on buck sweep.

3) Widen his splits by alignment.

4) Run "trade" and move your TE/Wing away from him pre-snap.

Terms

Head Up – The defensive lineman has lined up directly in front of and offensive lineman.

Shade – The defensive lineman is lined up in a gap between offensive linemen.

Stance – How each linemen will be set before the ball is snapped.

Leverage – Understanding the angles and where to move.

Down – Blocking the first thing inside.

Out – Blocking the first thing outside.

Stay – Do not pull that is tagged for a lineman on a play.

Path – The track of the lineman on a down block or wrap.

Kick – To block the end man out.

Log – To wrap the end man on the line and seal him in.

Wrap – Working to a second level linebacker on the other side of the center.

Conclusion

 # **Conclusion**

I want to thank you for your support of my materials. This offense has served me well for many years, but like any offense it needs to continue to grow and evolve. So use this book as a guide and please reach out to let me know how it is going at your school if you choose to install it.

The coaching community is a great community to be a small part of and I am beyond surprised with the response I have received.

For those of you interested:

The entire system can be found on Coachtube.com:

There is also more information on my website: FBCoachsimpson.com

Feel free to also reach out with questions: FBCoachSimpson@gmail.com

Coach Simpson
Find A Way

About The Author

Coach Simpson is currently the Head Football Coach at Searcy High School, a 6A school in Arkansas. Before taking the job at Searcy, Simpson was the Head Football Coach at Southside High School, a 4A school in Arkansas. Taking over a program that had won eight games in five seasons and had been on a 20+ game losing streak, Simpson has led Southside to the playoffs for four-consecutive seasons and won two conference titles in the past three seasons. For his efforts, he was named 4A-2 Conference Coach of the Year (2017), named to the as a finalist for Hooten's Coach of the Year (2017) and has been the All-Star Nominee for the 4A-2 (2016 and 2019).

This is Coach Simpson's 4th book. He was a best-selling author for his first work <u>Find a Way: What I Wish I'd Known When I Became a Head Football Coach</u>. The book was released in 2019 and is available on <u>FBCoachSimpson.com</u>. It has sold over 2300 copies as of 2020. This is also the 2.0 version of the GUN-T-RPO offense. The first book has already sold over 1000 copies in just 6 short months.

About The Author

Simpson also raised over $1.5 million for Southside during his 9 seasons and has overseen several major facility projects including: New Field Turf, Expansion to Fieldhouse, Expansion to the school's home bleachers, and the addition of a press box and a new video-board.

Prior to coming to Southside, Simpson took over as Head Coach at Alabama Christian Academy in Montgomery, Alabama. During his tenure there, Simpson took over a team that had been 4-18 and led them to their first home playoff game in over 20-years. For his efforts he was named Montgomery Advertiser's All-Metro Coach of the Year as well as being voted 4A Region 2 Coach of the Year (2010). Simpson also served as the head track coach at ACA and led the girl's and boy's teams to multiple top 10 finishes in 4A.

About The Author

Simpson began his coaching career at Madison Academy, in Huntsville, Alabama. He served as a junior high basketball and football coach, before working into a varsity coaching role in football. He graduated from Harding University in 2003. He is married to Jamey and has three children: Avery, Braden and Bennett. The couple was married in 2001 after meeting at Harding University.

Contact Coach Simpson

@FBCoachSimpson – Twitter

Kenny Simpson – Facebook

FBCoachSimpson.com

Made in the USA
Columbia, SC
08 January 2025